The · Life Cycle · Series

The Life Cycle of a

RACCOON

John Crossingham & Bobbie Kalman

Illustrations by Barbara Bedell

 Crabtree Publishing Company

www.crabtreebooks.com

The Life Cycle Series

A Bobbie Kalman Book

Dedicated by John Crossingham
For Sarah Elizabeth Ingham—welcoming my first niece to the world

Editor-in-Chief
Bobbie Kalman

Writing team
John Crossingham
Bobbie Kalman

Editorial director
Niki Walker

Editors
Amanda Bishop
Rebecca Sjonger

Research
Ed Butts

Art director
Robert MacGregor

Design
Katherine Kantor
Margaret Amy Reiach (cover)

Production coordinator
Heather Fitzpatrick

Photo researcher
Laura Hysert
Crystal Foxton

Consultant
Patricia Loesche, Ph.D., Animal Behavior Program,
Department of Psychology, University of Washington

Photographs:
Frank S. Balthis: page 22
Erwin & Peggy Bauer: pages 12, 13 (bottom), 20, 23 (bottom), 26
Ivy Images: Bill Ivy: pages 13 (top), 18, 23 (top), 24 (bottom)
Robert McCaw: pages 3, 8 (bottom), 10, 15, 16 (bottom),
  19 (bottom), 21, 24 (top), 29 (top)
McDonald Wildlife Photography: Joe McDonald: page 27 (top)
Photo Network: James A. Hodnick: page 28
Allen Blake Sheldon: page 29 (bottom)
Tom Stack & Associates: Thomas Kitchin: pages 7, 8 (top),
  14, 17, 19 (top), 27 (bottom), 31 (top); Brian Parker: page 11;
  Victoria Hurst: pages 30, 31 (bottom)
Other images by Digital Stock, Adobe, and Corbis Images

Illustrations:
All illustrations by Barbara Bedell except the following:
Margaret Amy Reiach: border
Katherine Kantor: pages 6, 26 (right)
Bonna Rouse: page 17

Crabtree Publishing Company

www.crabtreebooks.com   1-800-387-7650

PMB 16A	612 Welland Avenue	73 Lime Walk
350 Fifth Avenue	St. Catharines	Headington
Suite 3308	Ontario	Oxford
New York, NY	Canada	OX3 7AD
10118	L2M 5V6	United Kingdom

Cataloging-in-Publication Data
Crossingham, John
  The life cycle of a raccoon / John Crossingham & Bobbie Kalman;
Illustrations by Barbara Bedell
    p. cm. -- (The life cycle series)
Includes index.
Explains the stages of raccoon development from birth to maturity,
including how cubs learn to forage, how they survive in cities, and
what human-made dangers they face.
  ISBN 0-7787-0661-3 (RLB) -- ISBN 0-7787-0691-5 (pbk.)
  1. Raccoons--Juvenile literature. [1. Raccoons.] I. Kalman, Bobbie.
II. Title. II. Series.
  QL737.C26C76 2003
  599.76'32--dc21
                                                                  2003002479
                                                                         LC

Contents

What is a raccoon?

Raccoons are **mammals**. All mammals breathe with lungs and have backbones. Mammals have bodies that are covered with fur or hair. They are **warm-blooded** animals, which means their bodies stay the same temperature in both hot and cold surroundings. Mothers give birth to **live young**. Baby mammals drink milk that is made in their mothers' bodies.

Raccoons are **nocturnal**, or active mainly at night. They often spend the night **foraging**, or searching for food. Raccoons are not picky eaters. They are **omnivores**, which means they eat both plants and animals. They use their excellent senses of sight, smell, hearing, and touch to find food.

Raccoons are well known for their markings—black "masks" on their faces and rings on their tails.

Raccoon relatives

Raccoons belong to a small family of mammals called *Procyonidae*. The other members of this family include coatis, ringtails, kinkajous, and olingos. There are seven **species**, or types, of raccoons. This book discusses the best-known raccoon species in North America—the common raccoon. The name "raccoon" comes from the Algonquian word "arakum." It means "he who scratches with his hands."

The South American crab-eating raccoon has shorter fur than the common raccoon has. Its strong jaws are perfect for crushing crab shells.

The kinkajou, shown here, and its cousin the olingo have small ears and thick, short fur. Both live in Central and South American forests. The kinkajou is larger than the olingo.

Scientists are still debating whether or not the red panda of Asia is a true raccoon relative.

Coatis are found mostly in Central and South America. They are excellent climbers and sleep in trees.

Ringtails live in Mexico and the southwestern United States. They are also called ring-tailed cats.

Where do raccoons live?

The purple area shows where raccoons live in North America.

Raccoons live in North and South America. They are found mostly in the eastern parts of the United States and Canada. The most common raccoon **habitats**, or home environments, are forests and wetlands, but raccoons also live on plains and in **urban** areas such as cities and towns.

Home, sweet home

Within their habitats, raccoons find snug **dens**, or homes, in which they sleep, hide from **predators**, and escape from harsh weather. Raccoons may have several homes at the same time. Instead of building dens, they use whatever spaces they can find, such as small caves or holes dug by other animals. Holes in large trees are popular spots because they are off the ground and away from predators. In urban areas, raccoons make their dens in chimneys, attics, abandoned cars, and basements.

Wetlands such as marshes are excellent raccoon habitats. They have plenty of plants and small animals for raccoons to hunt.

Forests and streams

Whenever possible, raccoons live near trees and rivers, streams, or lakes. Trees provide these animals with shelter and with fruits and nuts to eat. Raccoons are excellent swimmers and often hunt in water for small animals. They also drink the water and use it to soften their food before eating.

Different climates

Raccoons can live in many **climates**. Some live in areas with **tropical** climates, which are hot all year. Others live in places with **temperate** climates. Temperate areas have hot summers and cold winters.

The best raccoon habitats have safe spots for dens and steady supplies of food and clean water.

7

What is a life cycle?

The first two years of a raccoon's life are the most difficult. During this time, predators and diseases are major threats to these animals.

All animals go through a series of **stages**, or changes, known as a **life cycle**. The cycle begins when an animal is born. The animal moves through different stages as it grows and changes. Finally, it becomes an adult that can have babies of its own. Each baby starts a new life cycle. A raccoon's life cycle is similar to that of most mammals.

Life span

Animals also have **life spans**. A life span is the length of time an animal lives. Raccoons have different life spans depending on where they live. A raccoon living in the wild has a life span of five to eight years. Raccoons living in **captivity**, such as in zoos, can live between eight and thirteen years. Raccoons have longer life spans in captivity because they are not hunted by predators.

A raccoon living in the wild usually has a shorter life span than a raccoon in captivity has.

Life cycle of a raccoon

Raccoon **embryos**, or developing babies, grow inside their mothers until they are ready to be born. The babies are born together in **litters**, or groups. The baby raccoons, called **kits**, rely on their mothers for food and protection. At two to four months of age, a kit becomes a **juvenile**.

It is able to find its own food, but it still lives with its mother. By one year of age, a juvenile is almost its full adult size. It is now known as a **yearling**, or a year-old raccoon. The yearling leaves its mother to live on its own. A raccoon becomes a fully grown adult at around two years of age.

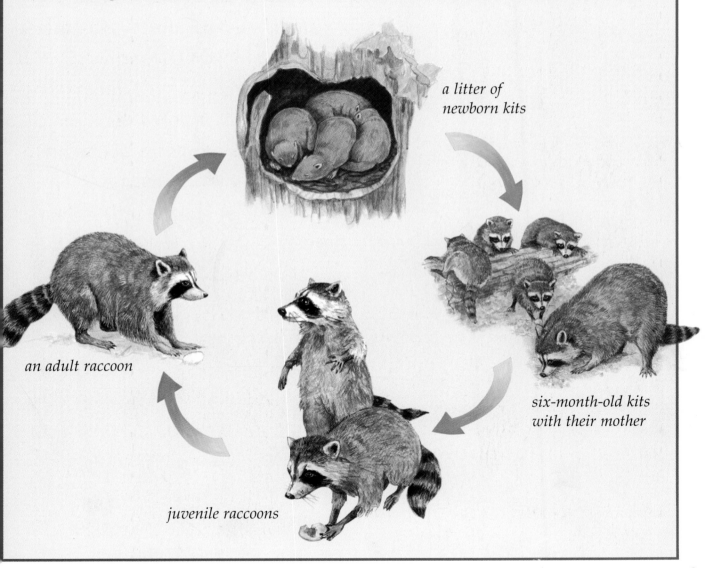

a litter of newborn kits

six-month-old kits with their mother

an adult raccoon

juvenile raccoons

9

Preparing for birth

This hole makes a great nursery den because it is high off the ground.

Male and female raccoons must **mate** in order to **reproduce**. They usually mate between January and March. Females give birth in April or May. Before a mother gives birth, her embryos **gestate**, or develop inside her body, for about nine weeks.

Get out!

A female raccoon may share her den with other adults, especially in winter. When she is ready to mate, however, she chases out the other raccoons and waits for a suitable male. Once the female is **pregnant**, she must prepare a snug and secure **nursery den**, in which she will give birth and raise her kits. If her den is in a tree, she may chew up and scratch the wood to make a soft floor for her kits. If her old den is not hidden well enough to protect her kits, she will find a new one.

Eating for a litter

Raccoons often have difficulty finding food during the winter, so they are hungry when spring arrives. Pregnant females are especially hungry. They need to eat more food than usual to help their embryos grow. They forage almost constantly in the spring.

The kits are born

Female raccoons give birth to one litter a year. Most raccoon litters have three to four kits. Some litters have as many as eight. The kits are born inside the nursery den. They are tiny and helpless. Their mother licks her babies clean as soon as they are born.

Newborn kits are only four to six inches (10-15 cm) long and cannot yet see or hear. They have only a thin layer of grayish fur. Their fur coat grows in a few weeks later. Often, kits are born without face and tail markings, which appear after a week.

For the first three weeks after birth, the eyes and ears of the kits are sealed.

Their first meal

Soon after they are born, kits begin drinking their mother's milk. The mother lies on her side or back to make it easy for them to reach her **teats**. This type of feeding is called **nursing**. Although they cannot see or hear, the kits can make noises. Newborns make high-pitched sounds similar to those made by chirping birds. They use these sounds to let their mother know that they are hungry.

A kit's teeth do not appear until the kit is one month old. It does not need teeth to nurse.

Kits cannot walk right away. They can use their hind legs to push themselves around, but their mother does not allow them to leave the den for several weeks.

Life with Mom

Most raccoons forage all night, but a new mother leaves her den for only a few hours each evening. She goes to places where she can find food quickly.

Kits spend their first few weeks sleeping and nursing. They have a lot of growing to do before their mother will allow them to leave the den. She rarely leaves them alone. She keeps a constant lookout for predators such as owls and foxes.

Quick growers

Kits grow quickly because their mother's milk is rich in fat and **nutrients**. By one month of age, the kits are more than twice the size they were when they were born. They can see and hear, and they can make a lot of sounds, too. Month-old kits growl, hiss, snort, and **chur**. A churring sound is similar to a cat's purr. Raccoons make this sound to comfort one another or to show that they are happy.

A mother is very protective of her small kits. She is careful to keep the kits out of harm's way.

The second month

During its second month, a kit begins to move a lot more. By six weeks of age, it can walk, run, and climb. Eventually, the kit begins to "play fight" with its brothers and sisters. The kits imitate **threat postures**, which are poses that adults use to scare away predators (see page 24). Play fighting helps kits get used to their bodies before they leave their mother.

Almost ready

The kits continue to drink milk for about two months. Eventually, their mother begins nursing them sitting up instead of lying down. If the kits are too small to reach her teats, she holds the babies up to them. When the kits are seven or eight weeks old, the mother moves them from the nursery den. She carries them one at a time to another one of her dens.

By the time a kit is two months old, its face mask and tail rings have grown in fully. Its body has also filled out. The kit looks like a tiny version of its parents.

Let's explore!

Once the young kits move to a new den, their lives start to change. Their mother begins to **wean** them, or stop feeding them her milk. By about three months of age, the young raccoons are juveniles. It is time for them to leave the den and learn to forage with their mother.

Follow me

Juveniles follow their mother in single file as they forage. The mother churs to them so that they stay close to her. It is important for the group to keep together because young raccoons are still easy **prey** for predators. When a juvenile tries to wander away, its mother swats it and brings it back to the group. If danger is near, she grunts loudly.

Juveniles know how to climb up trees (top), but they need their mother (bottom) to teach them how to get down again!

What's on the menu?

A mother teaches her juveniles how to find all sorts of food. She shows them which bark, berries, and nuts are good to eat. She also teaches them how to hunt animals such as frogs, snails, insects, and small fish. Reptile and bird eggs are another important food.

Using their excellent sense of smell and their sharp claws, juveniles learn how to find a turtle's buried nest and dig up the eggs.

Just add water

Raccoons usually eat near water. In fact, people used to think that raccoons washed their food before they ate it. They do not wash their food, however—they use water to soften it. Raccoons also dip their **forepaws**, or front paws, into the water. They have very sensitive skin on their forepaws, and it becomes even more sensitive when it is wet. Juveniles learn to wet their forepaws while eating. They then use them to feel the food and find the right parts to eat.

*Raccoons are skilled at catching fish and other **aquatic**, or water-dwelling, prey. Mothers teach these skills to their young.*

17

Home range

A male raccoon fiercely defends his home range against other males.

Every raccoon has a **home range**, or an area in which the animal has its dens and forages for food. Even raccoons that live in cities or towns have home ranges. Raccoons rarely leave their home ranges unless they can no longer find food or suitable mates.

How big?

The size of a raccoon's home range depends on how much food is available there. The more there is to eat, the smaller the home range is because the raccoon does not have to travel very far to find food. In some areas a raccoon may need only an area the size of a football field for its range. The largest raccoon home ranges are around three square miles (8 square km).

Familiar ground

A raccoon stays in its home range because it is safest there. It knows everything about the area, such as exactly where to find food and water. It also knows the best spots for dens and the safest places to take daytime naps. When a raccoon senses danger, it does not have to search for a place to hide—it already knows where to go to escape from predators.

Male and female raccoon home ranges usually overlap. Some raccoons even share the same den or help one another find food.

*Raccoons that live in urban areas often have **routes**, or paths, that they follow over and over again while foraging. Each route leads to a favorite feeding place.*

Leaving home

When juveniles are four or five months of age, they become more independent. They begin to sleep and forage on their own. The juveniles are not yet fully grown, but they have learned a lot about finding food and escaping from predators. Eventually, they leave their mother's den and range to find home ranges of their own.

Time to go

The time when a juvenile leaves its mother depends on where it lives. Raccoons that live in places with warm winters often leave home during their first autumn, when they are five to seven months old. Juveniles in colder areas, such as Canada and the northern United States, stay near their mothers until they are almost a year old. They wait until spring arrives before searching for a new home.

If there is a steady supply of food, some juvenile females stay on the home ranges of their mothers. Males always leave to find new home ranges.

The search is on

Male juveniles travel farther than females do when they look for home ranges. Males must find areas that are not already taken by adult male raccoons. Adult males usually do not let others into their home ranges. If they did, they would have more competition while searching for mates. A male travels between ten and twenty miles (16 to 32 km) in search of his new home range. A female often travels only a short distance from her mother's range. She is not likely to be driven out of an area by an adult raccoon unless there is a shortage of food.

The strongest juveniles in a litter usually get a home range close to where they were born. The weaker litter mates are driven farther away. This juvenile looks comfortable in its new home.

Making babies

A raccoon can reproduce when it is **mature**, or fully grown. Females are ready to mate at about one year of age. Males take longer to mature. They must grow bigger so they will be strong enough to compete with other males for mates. Most males are ready to reproduce at two years of age.

Finding a mate

When a male is ready to mate, he must search for a female. He knows where females have dens in his home range. If there are few or no females in his area, he leaves his home range to find a mate. He uses his sense of smell to find females who are in **estrus**, or ready to mate. He will mate with as many females as he can.

February is the most common month for males to look for mates.

Not so fast

Female raccoons are choosy about their partners. They are aggressive toward any males that approach them. They growl and try to drive the males away. Weak males are frightened away, but strong males persist. This process ensures that only the strongest males will be the fathers of kits.

Males make a "whoo" sound to attract attention when they are looking for a mate.

Time together

After mating, a male and female stay together for up to a month. During this time, the male sleeps in the female's den and forages with her. Eventually, the male leaves her den. While he may try to find another female in estrus, she may search for a nursery den. The pregnant female will not let another raccoon into her den until her kits are born.

During mating season, male raccoons are aggressive and always watchful for the presence of other males.

Sending messages

When in danger, adults growl and hiss to scare away enemies. They grunt or scream to warn other raccoons to find shelter fast.

Raccoons **communicate**, or send messages, in many ways. They use sounds, body positions, and scents to send messages to raccoons and other animals. For example, kits make various cries and chirps to let their mother know they are hungry or cold.

Stay away!

An aggressive raccoon uses threat postures to frighten away predators or other raccoons. It turns back its ears and flattens them against its head. It bares its teeth and keeps its head low. Finally, it thrashes its tail back and forth.

What's that smell?

Each raccoon has a slightly different scent. A raccoon rubs itself against trees and rocks in its home range to leave its scent in the area. Its scent warns other raccoons: "This place is taken—find your own home!" Raccoons also use their strong sense of smell to help recognize each other and to locate their kits.

Good night

Raccoons living in areas with cold winters face low temperatures and a lack of food. They survive this difficult season by entering a state of deep sleep called **torpor**. To prepare for this sleep, raccoons spend the autumn eating as much fatty food as they can find. The food gets stored in their bodies as fat, so the raccoons do not have to forage much in the winter. Instead, they can sleep in their winter dens and live off the energy stored in their body fat.

Quick risers

Torpor is similar to another type of deep sleep called **hibernation**, but a hibernator does not wake up at all during winter. Its body temperature drops to just above freezing. It takes a few days for a hibernating animal to wake up fully. An animal that enters torpor, such as a raccoon or a bear, can wake up very quickly if it needs to. Its body temperature drops only a few degrees. It enters torpor only on the coldest days. On warm days, the animal leaves its den to forage or even find a mate.

Remarkable raccoons

Raccoons are well **adapted** to their habitats. Their bodies are designed to help them find food, avoid predators, and raise young. These pages show some of the many things that make raccoons remarkable animals.

Hiding out

A raccoon's colors and markings act as **camouflage**. They help the animal blend in with its surroundings. A raccoon is difficult to spot when it sits still among trees. Its fur is similar in color to tree bark, and its face mask and tail rings look like the shadows of branches.

Good hands

Raccoons have well-developed forepaws compared to those of other animals. Raccoon forepaws are very flexible and can firmly grasp objects as small as a dime. Their palms are also extremely sensitive, especially when they are wet. Raccoon palms can feel small vibrations in the water made by prey such as fish, crabs, or crayfish.

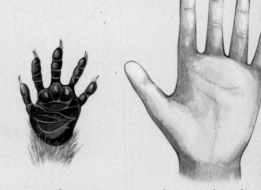

raccoon forepaw　　*human hand*

Keeping things clean

Raccoons that live in the same home range leave their droppings in a shared pit called a **latrine**. This behavior keeps their dens clean. Raccoons sometimes identify others in their home range by the smell of their droppings.

I can get in there!

Raccoons are intelligent animals that are able to learn quickly. They are especially curious when it comes to finding food. Raccoons can figure out how to open doors, cupboards, garbage cans, and refrigerators when there is food to be found. They can even use pet doors to get into homes.

Chomp, chomp

Raccoons inspect their food closely before eating it. They shake their food in water, rub it with their forepaws, and place it right against their noses to sniff it.

Life near water gives raccoons opportunities to eat and to explore.

Dangers to raccoons

Even though raccoons are strong and intelligent, they still face many dangers. Some threats, such as illnesses, are natural. Sadly, however, most of the dangers raccoons face are caused by humans. Pollution, car collisions, hunting, and the loss of habitats all endanger the lives of raccoons.

When cutting down trees to make paper or wood, companies often **clear-cut**, or take down all the trees in an area. This practice destroys raccoon habitats. Raccoons need trees for food and shelter, as shown above. When trees in a raccoon's home range are cleared, the animal must leave its home.

Hunters

Raccoons must always watch out for predators such as alligators, foxes, wolves, and owls. The most dangerous hunters, however, are people. People hunt raccoons for their fur and sometimes just for sport.

Road hazard

In some areas, more raccoons are killed by cars than by anything else. Most victims are young raccoons that do not yet realize the dangers of roads and cars.

This raccoon was caught in an urban area by an animal control officer. It will be returned to the wild.

That stinks!

Air and water pollution hurts all animals, including raccoons. The plants that raccoons eat do not grow well when the air is polluted. Water pollution is even more harmful because raccoons feed on many animals that live in water. The prey animals take in pollution from the water, and it gets passed on to the raccoons that eat them. Raccoons also drink the polluted water and use it to soften their food.

Helping raccoons

One of the best ways to help raccoons is to respect their environment. Recycling glass, plastic, metal, and paper products reduces pollution. Supporting groups that oppose clear-cutting also helps preserve the trees raccoons need to survive.

Raccoons may look cuddly, but they are wild animals. They may bite when approached or threatened, and their bites can pass on diseases such as rabies. If you find a raccoon, just let it be. Do not try to touch it! Never feed a raccoon or keep one as a pet.

You have to leave

Raccoons often use parts of houses and sheds as dens. Close up any crawl spaces to keep raccoons out. If you do discover a raccoon living on your property, call your local animal control center to remove the animal and return it safely to the wild.

Don't tempt me

A raccoon living in or near a city will come back to places where it knows it can get food. Do not leave pet food where raccoons can get it. Raccoons are well known for knocking over garbage cans to find food, so make sure your family has cans with locking lids. If a raccoon cannot find any food in your area, it will not bother your home.

Raccoons love finding food left out by people. If a raccoon gets your food, do not try to take the food away!

Glossary

Note: Boldfaced words defined in the book may not appear in the glossary.

adapted To be suited to a certain habitat or environment

captivity A confined space that is removed from the wild

climate The long-term weather conditions in an area, including temperature, rainfall, and wind

estrus The period of time during which a female is ready to mate

live young Describing a baby animal that does not hatch from an egg

mate To join together to make babies

nutrient A substance that living things need for growth and good health

nursery den A den in which a mother raccoon gives birth and raises her kits

predator An animal that hunts and eats other animals

pregnant Describing a female animal that has one or more babies growing inside her

prey An animal that is hunted and eaten by other animals

reproduce To make babies

teat A nipple on a female mammal through which a baby drinks milk

Index

1 2 3 4 5 6 7 8 9 0 Printed in the U.S.A. 2 1 0 9 8 7 6 5 4